AN OMNIBUS/PUFFIN BOOK

A PADDOCK *of* POEMS

Have you ever bought a secondhand dragon? Have you ever made a voyage in a waterbed, heard letters gossiping in a mailbag, or had a dinosaur knock at your door? Have you ever gone mad doing a school project or mixed the mayonnaise with the sunburn cream?

In this first Omnibus Puffin selection of Australian Poets, Max Fatchen explores all these situations and more. Some poems in this book will make you shriek, but others will make you sit back and dream of a creek that sings, a tide that talks, and a telltale breeze that whispers at your window.

For my grandchildren Jessica, Nicholas, Dominic, Jonathan, Claire and Sarah and for my friends next-door, Annmarie, Tommy, André, Raymond, Matthew, Janine and Anne-Marie and also for Pauline Fietz, not forgetting Magoo, the dog, and Rufus the cat.

Cover and text illustrations by Kerry Argent
Edited by Celia Jellett

A PADDOCK *of* POEMS

Max Fatchen

AN OMNIBUS/PUFFIN BOOK

Omnibus Books
9 Edward Street
Adelaide, South Australia, 5000
Australia

Penguin Books Australia Ltd,
487 Maroondah Highway, P.O. Box 257
Ringwood, Victoria, 3134, Australia
Penguin Books Ltd,
Harmondsworth, Middlesex, England
Penguin Books,
40 West 23rd Street, New York, N.Y. 10010 U.S.A.
Penguin Books Canada Limited,
2801 John Street, Markham, Ontario, Canada L3R 1B4
Penguin Books (N.Z.) Ltd.
182–190 Wairau Road, Auckland 10, New Zealand

Published by Penguin Books Australia Ltd in association
with Omnibus Books, 1987
Copyright © Max Fatchen 1987
Illustrations copyright © Omnibus Books 1987

"Dinosaur Department" was first published in *Digging up the Past*
(Expressway Readers) and is reprinted by arrangement with
Jacaranda Wiley Ltd

Typeset in Australia by Caxtons Pty Ltd, Adelaide
Made and printed in Australia by The Book Printer,
Maryborough, Victoria

CIP

Fatchen, Max
   A paddock of poems.
   For children.
   ISBN 0 14 032476 3.
   1. Country life — Juvenile poetry. 2. Children's poetry,
   Australian. I. Title. (Series: Omnibus/Puffin poetry).
A821'.3

Contents

Our paddock of poems
Has thundering herds
Of dinosaurs, dragons
And galloping words.
We'll capture a couplet,
Or, if you have time,
We'll land you a limerick
Or round up a rhyme.
Be wary of creatures
That rhymsters produce,
And saddle your stanzas,
A poet is loose!

Summer Mail

The country mail is coming
Across the wilting land,
Through summer's dancing hazes
And slyly shifting sand.

The country mailman's whistling,
With elbow out the side,
His dog upon the mailbag
With watchful canine pride.

And while the mail truck's jolting
Where stony creekbed shelves,
You'll hear the mail bag's letters
All talk among themselves . . .

. . . "We've added to the kitchen
And thanks for sending cups . . .
"Belinda's had her baby . . .
The heeler's had her pups . . .

. . . "The shearing shed's got termites . . .
We wondered if you'd heard . . ."
The letters go on talking
With word on whispered word . . .

"It's lonely in the city . . .
For home a bloke gets sick . . .
"I hear the bull took after Mum . . .
I'm glad that she was quick . . .

"I miss the country mornings . . .
I miss my old straw hat . . ."
The mailman keeps on driving
While still the letters chat.

. . . "Dear Sir, on payment of account
We felt we should enquire,
A box of nails, two milking pails . . .
A roll of fencing wire . . ."

. . . "Dear Gran, will you remember,
That I'll be eight next week . . ."
The mailman's truck is grinding
Across another creek.

While letter after letter
Recites its humble tale,
That's if you dare to listen
To bags that carry mail.

The mailman's reached the township
His old truck starts to slow.
A world is in his mailbag.
I wonder does he know?

In a whirl

Willy-nilly, round and round,
Whirlwind swirling from the ground,
Picking up its bits of paper,
In a skywards-spinning caper.
With a whistle and a howl,
Waltzing with a squawking fowl,
Snatching clothes from whizzing line.
Some of them, I fear, are mine.

Slamming doors and rattling tin
Goes this windy larrikin.
Joyous in the air it flings
Multitudes of dizzy things,
Shoals of leaves from blowing boughs,
Hats it snatched from children's brows,
Wrapped around with dusty banners,
Whirlwinds have such awful manners.

Thieving, swirling tower of dirt,
You went and stole my Sunday shirt.

Windy Work

Weary breeze through my window screen,
Where are you going and where have you been?

. . . I cooled the sweat on a farmer's brow
And fanned the dreams of a dozing cow.
I played a tune in the telephone wires
And rocked the trees for the magpie choirs.
I shook the stalks of the long-eared wheat
And they danced the paddock off its feet.

I passed a train with its diesel smell.
I caught the clang of the crossing bell.
I tumbled the bushes and made them roll
And fluttered the flag on a schoolyard pole.
I carried the children's lunch-hour shout
No wonder a breeze is a bit puffed out.

I rushed and rippled a placid dam.
I stroked the grass and here I am.
I climbed the range and each rock-ridged hill.
So may I rest on your windowsill?

At Sunrise

Across the silent paddock
There comes a cautious hare,
His ears, two pointed fingers,
To probe the frosty air.
And where the wheat is growing
He pauses in his run
Along the aisles of morning,
To breakfast with the sun.

Precious

On webs the evening spiders spun
The drops of dew now catch the sun,
In shining strands they glisten there,
Those morning pearls my fences wear.

Plough Song

The old plough is singing its song in the rain,
The turning of earth and the growing of grain,
The life that can spring from the uprooted clods
Where slowly and surely the heavy horse plods.

The roar of the tractor, the turn of a disc . . .
Where farming's a science the sowing is brisk
Replacing the horse with a star on its brow
Majestically hauling its labouring plough.

But clattering levers, the sway and the swing
Where slow teams went plodding when horses were king,
Had the rhythm of seasons where toiling heads bowed
And paddocks would breathe in the furrows they ploughed.

The tractor cab's muted with hardly a sound
Of the soil that will break in the song of the ground.
With ghostly persistence, when dreams will allow,
They pass in the distance . . . the horse and the plough.

Sounds

Clang and bang the hammer head goes
Where the bellows huff to its lusty blows
And fierce and red the forge fire glows
To the sound of the metal ringing.
Where horseshoes shape in their shining arc
While hammers dance with the spurting spark
The toil of teams from dawn to dark
Is there in the anvil's singing.

Gate Gossip

I like our gate,
Its sturdy charm
That guards the entrance
To our farm.

It's nice when shut,
Or open wide,
To sit upon
Or sit astride.

But gates are there
With things to do
Like letting sheep
And cattle through.

Our gate has bars
With several bends
From careless cars
Of farming friends.

The gateposts lean,
A little tired,
With fences stretching
Rusty-wired.

A country gate
Is surely best
To prop a farmer
For his rest.

With one foot up,
And elbows flat
Now who could pass
A man like that?

While every bit
Of iron will ring,
With all the
Rural gossiping.

The magpies fly
To sunset tree.
A voice impatient
Calls to tea.

Then, whistling,
Home the farmer goes
As gate
And conversation
Close.

The Milker

Up and down,
Squeeze and squirt,
Milky splashes
On my shirt.
Tug and press,
Down and up,
Creamy streams
For can and cup.
Custards, puddings,
Ice cream, cheese,
Brim the bucket
at my knees.
Milky marvel,
Tasty tides.
Praise the cow
And her insides.

Down and up,
Squirt and squeeze.
(Mine's a chocolate malted,
Please.)

Calling all Cars

All areas were notified.
It seemed a puzzling case.
The raspberry ripple ice cream tub
Had vanished without trace.

A tub of most exquisite brand
And only newly bought.
Identikits were quickly scanned
And witnesses were sought.

The motive? It was surely greed
And those who probe and pry
Can be a shrewd and dogged breed
Who test each alibi.

For suddenly the breakthrough came
But only just in time.
Within an ear, a whispered name
Connected with the crime.

And so we happily report
That, by informers branded,
The criminal has now been caught
Red-raspberry-ripple-handed.

The Ballad of the Waterbed

I'll tell you a tale, a spanking yarn
And one to turn your head . . .
Of a boy's delight, how he sailed each night
On his wonderful waterbed.

A waterbed is a magical thing
But not for the timid soul.
It will plunge and lift as the dreamers drift
While the bedroom billows roll.

So he sailed away to a sandy cay
To the pirates' savage lair
Where the gun-lined hulls flew their cross-boned skulls
And gunsmoke filled the air.

He set his sheets for the plundering fleets
Where the victims screamed and bled
And the captains paled, for none outsailed
That scurvy waterbed.

Fierce Captain Kidd had dipped his lid
And Blackbeard cried, "It's daft,
I've never seen, in the Caribbean,
The likes of this 'ere craft."

With a swig of rum for his parrot chum
How Long John Silver roared.
But he quickly sank from a salt-stained plank
When he tried to climb aboard.

So the boy came back when the tide grew slack
To the morning clear and bright,
As he woke he said to the waterbed,
"We sail again tonight".

So woe to the landlubbers left behind . . .
No treasure or diamond rings
But high and dry with a jealous sigh
On their dull old innersprings.

But I'll tell you this . . . where the bow waves hiss
When the midnight's stroke has gone
Don't risk your neck on a waterbed deck
And keep your lifebelt on!

Silly Billy

When Billy blew his bubble gum
It grew like some enormous moon.
It lifted him with frightening speed,
A sticky and a green balloon.

So upwards, upwards Billy soared
Until he reached tremendous heights.
It broke all records they could find
For unrestricted bubble flights.

But I am very much afraid
The bubble burst, the gum was popped
And now they work with scoop and spade
To fill the hole where Billy dropped.

Indeed, I think the time has come
When you should act on this assumption,
That people, blowing bubble gum,
Should use a little bubble gumption.

Pudding Power

This story, not for foolish waster,
Concerns a leading pudding taster
To whom folk came from far and wide
And brought their puddings and their pride.

He tasted puddings small and neat
And others scarcely fit to eat,
While some had burnt obnoxious bumps
Or even worse—large, doughy lumps.
Each pudding he devoured with care.
No crumb would pudding taster spare.

His form grew round with spotty skin.
His trousers wouldn't keep him in,
Until, by pudding overloaded,
He not surprisingly exploded.

From what folk heard and what they saw
This sad conclusion one must draw:
That pudding freaks who feed their faces
Need pudding firmly in their places.

Happy Landing

Oh swifter than the speed of light,
It came from far galactic zones.
Computerised its lonely flight
Past old dead moons and planets' bones.

From hemispheres of gas and dust,
From blazing stars and boiling slime,
It flew, with overpowering thrust
And creatures of another time.

A ball of fire, a sizzling streak.
No interstellar ship was quicker.
It landed in our street this week
And promptly got a parking sticker.

Space Ace

I'm a space ace of skill and of daring.
The galaxies ring with my fame
And rows of bright medals I'm wearing.
Darth Vader turns pale at my name.

Superman is my friend and my ally,
And I think him a very nice bloke.
He flies in for supper on Sundays
With a swirl of his colourful cloak.

Fan letters from Venus and Saturn,
And here I'll be quoting a few:
"Dear Sir, I'm your greatest admirer.
Respectfully signed, Doctor Who."

I baffle the shrewdest commanders
And dodge interplanetary trap.
Molecular structures I shatter,
Rogue rockets I ruthlessly zap.

I'm the hero of comet and planet.
My lasers can win any war.
How come that I lose all the battles
With the teacher I have in Year Four?

Shakes and Ladders

As a leaning
 ladder
  climber
   there are careful
    steps to take.
     Surely nothing
      can be sadder
       if a careless
        move you make.
         Do not slither,
          Do not stumble
           or your nerves
            can come unstrung
             and you well
              may take
               a tumble
                if you miss
                 another rung.
                  If you're lost
                   upon a ladder
                    do not think
                     this statement
                      rude.
                       If you only
                        took
                         your bearings
                          you might learn
                           your
                            laddertude.

Down and up

Words top.
are very
nice the
to reach
speak you
and until
read stop
and never
some and
are along
very read
long so
indeed play
and to
if out
you come
are us
the like
reading words
age for
you'll way
reach different
the a
bottom quite
of going
this We're
page. Now read across. We'd like to say

Anyone wanting a fiery dragon?

With a sulphur smell,
The air grew hot
As the dragon steamed
On the used car lot.

"Genuine scales,
A spiky tail,"
The notice said,
"This beast for sale."

"Belches flame
In a crimson sheet,
And guarantees
A steady heat.

"Huge and fearless,
Brave and bold
And thermostatically
Controlled."

"It's careful not
To sear or scorch.
Use as a heater
Or a torch."

"Warmer than
A blacksmith's forge,
And recommended
By Saint George."

I bought the beast,
What else to do?
Now you should see
My barbecue!

Who's there?

If you hear a dinosaur
Knocking loudly on your door,
Through the keyhole firmly say
"Nobody is home today".
If the bell should start to ring,
Tell the beast, "No visiting".
If you see there's more than one,
Turn around and start to run.

Dinosaur Department

Clever Clem went out of doors,
Playing with the dinosaurs,
Telling others in his class,
"Not to worry. They eat grass."
A snap, a CRUNCH! The sad news breaks
That clever boys can make mistakes.

Brain Drain

The dinosaurs did not remain
Because they had a tiny brain.
But recently, our teacher found
That tiny brains are still around . . .

Is this yours?

The gecko sometimes sheds its tail
In danger or distress.
How careless of it not to leave
A forwarding address!

I say!

Cockatoos are talkative
And readily converse.
But words they speak
Through cheeky beak
Can go from bird to worse.

Just friends

A cockroach hasn't many friends
And neither has the rhino.
I know which one I'd sooner have
To live beneath our lino.

Crunchy

With all that morning fibre
And breakfast bran to greet me
I keep away from horses
In case they want to eat me!

You rang?

My father thinks the telephone
Is something better left alone.
His attitude? Do please excuse it.
He never gets a chance to use it.

Tide Talk

The tide and I had stopped to chat
About the waves where seabirds sat,
About the yachts with bobbing sails
And quite enormous, spouting whales.

The tide has lots to talk about.
Sometimes it's in. Sometimes it's out.
For something you must understand,
It's up and down across the sand;
Sometimes it's low and sometimes high.
It's very wet and never dry.

The tide, quite crossly, said: "The sea
Is always out there pushing me.
And just when I am feeling slack,
It sends me in then drags me back.
It never seems to let me go.
I rise. I fall. I'm to and fro."

I told the tide, "I know it's true
For I am pushed around like you.
And really do they think it's fair?
Do this. Do that. Come here. Go there."

Then loudly came my parents' shout.
So I went in.
                    The tide went out.

Playing Dirty

The Romans built their road and path
And also built the Roman bath.
Their enemies had little hope,
For what is worse than swords?
                    Why, soap.

What am I?

I can flap like a bat.
I can hug like a bear.
I can purr like a cat.
I can run like a hare.

I can roar like a lion.
I can hop like a flea.
I can eat like a horse
When I'm ready for tea.

But when I have meals,
And I'm eating a lot,
I'm something that squeals,
I'm a greedy young what . . .?

But why not?

She comes at four to rap the door
And asking who will play?
Please, Annmarie. It cannot be,
No visiting today.

For Lucy, with her homework,
Is making awful scenes,
While Martha's lumps could well be mumps
And Albert's split his jeans.

With Arthur's bathroom drawings
I'm not exactly smitten,
While mother cat, on our best mat
Has had another kitten.

The fridge has just defrosted.
The spuds are boiling dry.
That fearful, smoking ruin
Was once an apple pie.

The telephone keeps ringing,
The gurgling sink is blocked.
The car keys are . . . inside the car
Which now, alas, I've locked.

The kitchen is a bedlam.
So all that I can say,
No, Annmarie . . . WOE, Annmarie,
No visiting today.

How Awful

When Sarah holds her baby brother
The feeling in her arms is numbing.
She also mentions to his mother,
There's something faulty with his plumbing.

Do it yourself

"Oh please will you hold baby,
It's such a little dear."
But let them keep on asking,
For, frankly I stand clear . . .
That burping and that crowing
Well, this is how I view it,
It's bad enough just knowing
That I'm related to it.

Uncle Fred

Uncle Fred with glares and stitches
Constantly repairs his britches.
Though he tries a larger fitting
Uncle Fred is always splitting,
Every straining seam expanding,
All his efforts notwithstanding.

Oh the ripping and the rending.
More repairs, alas, are pending.
Fat men who insist on bending
Can't expect a happy ending.

Be warned

I always get into a stew
With people who read in the loo.
No wonder I rage
As they're turning each page
For the rest of us want to go, too.

Here, Puss

We have
a sitting-
straight
cat,
a trim
and tabby
friend.
Our cat
won't fuss.
She purrs at us and curls

one end
at
up

And s-s-so to b-b-bed

"Do go to bed," they're saying,
But do they know what's there,
Within that crowded darkness
Or shrieking through the air?

What's that upon the bedrail?
What's hiding underneath?
There could be miles of crocodiles
With big, expectant teeth.

"Now go to bed this instant!"
But have they ever dared
The shadows in the passageway?
Were parents *never* scared?

"Now into bed." Their voices
Are rising to a shout.
But when they turn the light off

It's then the *THINGS* come out!

Are you in there?

It's what I've been dreading
And who would rejoice
On hearing those footsteps
The tone in that voice?
And what to reply,
For it's laden with doom —
That terrible cry
"Have you tidied your room?"

Help!

Any magazines
With scenes
Or information
On transportation,
population,
inflation,
marine parks,
or sharks?
Any clues
or news
on political views
Or Who's Who's?

Anything about
statistics,
national characteristics,
mountain ranges,
climatic changes,
hiking
or the Viking?

Any slides
on tides,
wading birds,
herds
or Kurds?

What about
The race
in space,
flora,
or an aurora?

Any files
on crocodiles?

If you haven't looked
For goodness' sake, DO!

On Friday morning
My project's due.

Glassy stare

The large glass jars in our country store
Have jellybeans and mints,
While all around their sides are found,
Small, loving fingerprints.
With little dots and funny spots . . .
Forgive this smudgy mess
For that is where, from on a chair,
Our little noses press.

To wheel little kids in a trolley
In supermarts surely seems folly,
For they fasten themselves
On the merchandise shelves,
Each firmly attached to a lolly.

It's a puzzle

In the days of their youth, so my parents keep saying
They had all their duties and never much playing.

They never did funny old things to their hair
In the days of their youth, so my parents declare.
They say they are puzzled by tantrums and 'teens
And why I'm quite happy in faded blue jeans.
So what's going on with the young generation?
They're earnestly hoping for some explanation.

Well . . . ask me tomorrow. To tell you the truth
I'm too busy now with the days of my youth.

Night Cricket

Cricket at nights,
Beneath the lights
Before the shouting crowd.
The shriek, the squeal,
The fierce appeal
Alas, it's disallowed.

Cricket at night,
The ball in flight
And every fieldsman tense.
Square leg and slips
And Coke and chips
And banners on the fence.

More overthrows,
The chanting grows.
The pitch will take a thumping.
The keeper's glove
Will snatch and shove
To make another stumping.

The moon is high.
My mouth is dry
With eardrums nearly splitting.
The oval's green
But have you seen
Such hurricanes of hitting?

A sudden shout,
He's out. HE'S OUT!
And oh the crowd's delight.
Caught in the deep.
Who wants to sleep
With cricketing at night!

The Twelfth Man

I'm ALWAYS twelfth man
Though I do what I can
But somehow they never can see
That my spinners have turn
And I'm willing to learn.
It's strange that they never choose me.

I've taken a catch
In a very hard match.
I'm loudest when making appeals.
I think it a shame
As the hope of the game
I'm simply left kicking my heels.

You can always rely
That I'll save the leg bye.
I'm a player as cool as a cat.
Do you know what they DID,
Picked another daft kid,
Because of his quality bat?

So when I'm a star
Where the Test matches are,
The bowlers will tremble and pray.
WHAT, someone has mumps?
Oh bring out the stumps.
Hurray, I'll be playing today.

Another tie

Players careless with their laces
Often end with flattened faces.

Ouch

Meredith likes hockey.
She nearly always wins.
She's fast. She's tall.
She whacks the ball
And everybody's shins.

Whoa

Eleanor rides a piebald horse
That's very wise and knowing
And when it pulls up short . . . of course
Eleanor keeps on going.

Thud

The roller skates that Mary had
Were borrowed by her foolish dad.
He'll never make a brilliant skater,
Or so the doctor told us later.

At the beach

Our holiday activities
Have frantic, swimming strokes
With ice-creamed lips and sailing ships
And endless kiosk Cokes.
With sanded towels and gritty rugs
Among the seaside throngs
Where eager dogs mouth tennis balls
And people lose their thongs.
The mix-up with our salad lunch
We hardly like to raise,
The lettuce smeared with sunburn cream
Our backs with mayonnaise!

Wish you were here

We're sending you this saucy card
We hope you find it funny.
We'll also send you heaps of love
If you send heaps of money.

Our guest house has this one delight,
Banana custard every night.
No wonder, after such a meal,
I suddenly begin to peel.

Here's Albert in his bathers,
There isn't any doubt,
While some of him is in them,
That most of him is out.

Eric liked to spend the day
Eating at the takeaway.
But this was Eric's big mistake.
The chairs his weight began to break
Until, with pulleys and a derrick,
They had to takeaway poor Eric.

Iron Man

Proud on his board,
Surf wise and brave
There goes my father
Riding a wave.
A flurry of legs,
The sea in a lather,
And there goes the wave,
Riding my father.

Ski Run

Our water-skiing Susan's skill
Is full of grace and fast and free.
She's not a one for standing still
And skims across the startled sea.

She soars above the water jump
And in her clever, fearless way,
She's landing with a bounce and thump
To spangle all the air with spray.

She's laughing at her briny bath.
We hear her shrill, exultant shout.
She weaves a wide and rippled path
Behind the speeding runabout.

But look! She's whizzing for the land
And with a gritty hiss and crunch
She heads for me along the sand
And skis across my picnic lunch!

Sea Things

It may be stretching things a bit
But on this page an eel won't fit,
And that's because, it should be stated,
An eel is so darned eeeeeeeeeeeeeeeeeeeeeeeeeeeeeeeelongated.

The fiddler is a fish you'll see
With violin-like shape.
It's feeding in the shallows by
The headland and the cape.
The offspring often cause dismay
And even comments rude,
Their parents shouting in the spray,
"Stop fiddling with your food!"

When cockles see the sunrise,
Though watery, it's true,
They like to wake each other
With "Cockle-doodle-doo".

The hermit crab sneaks other shells.
In stolen premises it dwells.
But when approached by other hermits,
It wants to see their housing permits.

Big Mouth

The clam, it seems, is well equipped
For staying very tightly lipped
Although, about a year ago
One tried a rather curt "Hullo".
So now they've banned it from the rocks
For being such a chatterbox.

Games with names

Bedgerebong and Kooloonong
Take spelling that's adroit
While Kooweerup you should look up
Be careful with Koroit.
If La Perouse seems better news
Though some prefer Menangle,
A good hard look at Quambatook
May help you sort the tangle.
While Yackandandah's nice verandahs
Surround each pleasant villa
Dandongadale will make me pale —
I'm fine with Cowandilla.
Tangambalanga, Quorrobolong?
Pronouncing them I've tried.
I'll wait until, at Broken Hill,
They get my tongue untied.

54

A person from Indooroopilly
Has had a reception that's chilly.
Has anyone heard
Such a rhythmical word?
How dare he describe it as silly.

There was a young girl from Milang
Who hated the phone when it rang.
When awakened from slumber
By someone's wrong number
She used the most terrible slang.

Is Bendigo a place you know?
We hear reports are glowing.
We'll make a scene if you've not been.
Get Bendigo-go-going.

A drover from on the Barcoo
Made a self-raising damper that grew.
It's as big as a hill
And they're eating it still . . .
If only the story were true.

Creek Concert

Every night is a one-night stand
For the Bush Creek Frog and Mosquito Band
Where every frog is a baritone
While the creek performs on a musical stone.
The wind will strum in a well-tuned tree
Where an old mopoke is a bit off-key.
The moon will watch with one bright eye
From its private box in the upstairs sky.

The creekbed singer never tires
Where mosquitoes hum in ferocious choirs.
An owl drifts by in its watchful flight
On the vibrant air of melodious night.
A cricket chirps from a moonlit log
To harmonise with a solo frog
And through my window . . . splash! and plop!
The water music comes non-stop.

Original works by composers astute,
A scrub serenade for a hollow-branch flute
And drowsy songs of a dreaming land
By the Bush Creek Frog and Mosquito Band.

Dolphin Dizzy

The dolphins leapt with finny fuss
And spouted with a hiss of air.
They tantalised the octopus
While getting in the mermaids' hair.

Their language was a puzzling flow
Of funny little squeaks and squeals
As down and up and down they'd go,
Enjoying their extended meals.

So boisterous the dolphins' play,
The rushing of that riotous mob,
It made a nervous jellyfish,
A quivering, transparent blob.

The weary oysters in their beds
Of sleep, had not a single wink
While squid on seaweed letterheads
Wrote angry protests with their ink.

But then a cheer with peace at last!
The bay was free from dolphins' tricks,
For there are seven seas to sail.
They'd gone to find the other six!

Strictly for the birds

Our waterhole should suit quite well
The birds that seek a swish-sh-sh motel.
It's ideal as a stopping place
For herons with their stilt-like grace,
The surface smooth to land upon
For passing duck or weary swan.

A fine cuisine, secluded trees,
And yes, we have some vacancies.
No fancy frills, but nice and quiet.
Are frogs and crickets on your diet?
Or, if another dish you need,
We serve a juicy waterweed.

We like to set a decent tone
For feather bedding, bring your own.
A four star rating? Let us say
Our stars include the Milky Way
And while accommodation's damp
The moon can be your reading lamp.

Our hospitality's well meaning.
Facilities include dry preening
And, if you're only overnight,
We'll see you catch your early flight.

Silhouettes

I saw a swan in the evening glide
And then another by its side
Then came a line, a feathered fleet
That sailed where moon and water meet
As, one by one and bird by bird,
The glinting waves they gently stirred.
Across the lake their course they set,
Necks curving in a silhouette
Until I could not hear at all,
The drifting music of their call.
But when it came my time to sleep
I counted swans instead of sheep.

Children Lost

On a lonely beach the old wreck lies
With its rusted ribs and sides,
To the biting lash of the salty wind
And the drive of the flooding tides.

Years ago it was wrecked, they said,
Wrecked where the loud winds blew.
All hands were lost in the sad affair
And the women and children too.

It's there I went on a moonlit night
Where the cliffs slope wild and steep,
And suddenly came a shout and cry
As the ship awoke from sleep.

She had her masts and sails again,
No longer a broken wreck
While the sailors sang as they hauled the ropes
And the children played on the deck.

They shouted and played on the heaving deck
Or sat at their cabin tea
While the sly winds filled the swelling sails
On the toss of the cunning sea.

But no one knew and no one dreamed . . .
Beware of the sailor's boast
That says he's master of the sea
Or king of the rugged coast.

For I heard it all on a moonlit night,
The eager waves' wild roar
And the cries of the crew as the great sea threw
That broken ship ashore.

Where, where the children? Never a sound
On the reef's cold rock and stone
For the selfish sea had taken them all
And kept them for its own.

"Perhaps, perhaps . . .," the sea kings said
To the children deep and drowned,
"We will let you go to the shore again
But by this bond you're bound.

"That you are the children of the sea,
Of the waves and the dolphin's track
On a moonlit night we'll set you free
But then we'll call you back . . .

"On the ghostly beach you will play your games
But far from the cheerful town
Then back we'll call you, children, back
When the cold-eyed moon goes down."

Or so it seemed to come to me
In the voice of the wind and the tide
As I stood on the beach where the moonlight fell
On the ship with the broken side.

And did I hear and could I hear
The sound of some voices there?
Did figures form and vanish again
In the strange and haunted air?

How shall I tell you what I felt
And how will you understand
What, by the moon, my own eyes saw —
Small footprints in the sand!

About the Author

Max Fatchen was born on the Adelaide Plains and grew up on a farm among hayfields and huge Clydesdale horses which he drove in a plough, very crookedly. He later became a journalist, working on Adelaide newspapers, and travelled to many parts of Australia and overseas. He wrote stories about fishermen and the ships that supplied lighthouses, about the crews of outback trains, about atomic bombs, floods and fires. But he enjoyed writing about people most of all. He has written six novels, three books of verse and a collection of short stories. His verses are published in many British and Australian anthologies.

Max Fatchen was made a Member of the Order of Australia in 1980 for services to journalism and literature.

He has six grandchildren, who, he says, are kind to him, and with whom he likes to visit sweet shops and takeaways. He enjoys fishing, pondering, and parties where there are biscuits with hundreds and thousands embedded in their icing.